21st Century
Basic Skills
Library

KIDS CAN MAKE MANNERS COUNT
USE YOUR INDOOR VOICE!

NEPTUNE CITY
PUBLIC LIBRARY

3

by Katie Marsico

Cherry Lake Publishing • Ann Arbor, Michigan

Published in the United States of America
by Cherry Lake Publishing
Ann Arbor, Michigan
www.cherrylakepublishing.com

Content Adviser: Tonia Bock, PhD, Associate Professor of Psychology,
St. Thomas University, St. Paul, Minnesota

Photo Credits: Cover and pages 1, 4, 6, 8, 10, 12, 14, 18, and 20,
©Keri Langlois; page 16, ©SeanPavonePhoto/Shutterstock.com.

Library of Congress Cataloging-in-Publication Data
Marsico, Katie, 1980–
  Use your indoor voice! / by Katie Marsico.
    p. cm.—(21st century basic skills library) (Kids can make manners count)
  Includes bibliographical references and index.
  ISBN 978-1-61080-437-0 (lib. bdg.) — ISBN 978-1-61080-524-7 (e-book) —
ISBN 978-1-61080-611-4 (pbk.)
  1. Oral communication—Juvenile literature. I. Title.
  P95.M335 2013
  395.1'22—dc23   2012001711

Cherry Lake Publishing would like to acknowledge
the work of The Partnership for 21st Century Skills.
Please visit www.21stcenturyskills.org for more information.

Printed in the United States of America
Corporate Graphics Inc.
July 2012
CLFA11

TABLE OF CONTENTS

Bothering the Baby

Max and his dad liked to watch football on TV.

Max got excited during the games. He shouted and cheered!

Max had a little sister, Megan. She did not like all of the noise.

She woke up and cried every time Max yelled.

Making Manners Work

Max loved cheering for his favorite team.

Yet he did not like to see Megan upset.

Luckily, Max's dad had a good idea.

Max listened carefully to what his dad said.

Max's dad talked about using an indoor voice.

An indoor voice at certain times showed good **manners**.

Max often used his indoor voice during class.

He spoke up so his teacher and friends heard him.

Yet he saved all his shouting for recess.

When to Speak Softly

Max's dad said that being loud sometimes **bothered** other people.

His dad asked Max a question. When should Max use his indoor voice?

Max thought about when he used his indoor voice. He used it around people trying to **concentrate**.

He did not shout when he visited the library.

Max also used his indoor voice when someone was sleeping.

Soon he no longer yelled if Megan was napping.

Max began cheering more softly during football games.

Soon Megan started sleeping better.

Max still enjoyed watching football games with his dad.

Now he **practiced** better manners while having fun.

Find Out More

BOOK

Chancellor, Deborah. *Good Manners*. New York: Crabtree
  Publishing Company, 2010.

WEB SITE

**U.S. Department of Health and Human Services—
Building Blocks: Manners Quiz**
*www.bblocks.samhsa.gov/family/activities/quizzes/manners
.aspx*
Take a fun online quiz to test how much you know about
manners!

Glossary

bothered (BAH-thurd) hurt or upset

concentrate (KAHN-sun-trayt) to pay attention to something

manners (MA-nurz) behavior that is kind and polite

practiced (PRAK-tisd) did something regularly

Home and School Connection

Use this list of words from the book to help your child become a better reader. Word games and writing activities can help beginning readers reinforce literacy skills.

a	cried	idea	not	so	upset
about	dad	if	now	softly	use
all	did	indoor	of	someone	used
also	during	it	often	sometimes	using
an	enjoyed	library	on	soon	visited
and	every	like	other	speak	voice
around	excited	liked	people	spoke	was
asked	favorite	listened	practiced	started	watch
at	friends	little	question	still	watching
baby	football	longer	recess	talked	what
began	for	loud	said	teacher	when
being	fun	loved	saved	team	while
better	games	luckily	see	that	with
bothered	good	making	she	the	woke
bothering	got	manners	should	thought	work
carefully	had	Max	shout	time	yelled
certain	having	Max's	shouted	times	yet
cheered	he	Megan	shouting	to	
cheering	heard	more	showed	trying	
class	him	napping	sister	TV	
concentrate	his	noise	sleeping	up	

Index

About the Author

Katie Marsico is an author of children's and young-adult reference books. She lives outside of Chicago, Illinois, with her husband and children.